Guess Who?

By Susan Hall

National Library of Australia

Guess who?

I begin with  k

I eat eucalyptus leaves.

Guess who?

I begin with

I am one of the biggest
birds in the world, but
I can't fly.

Guess who?

I begin with  W

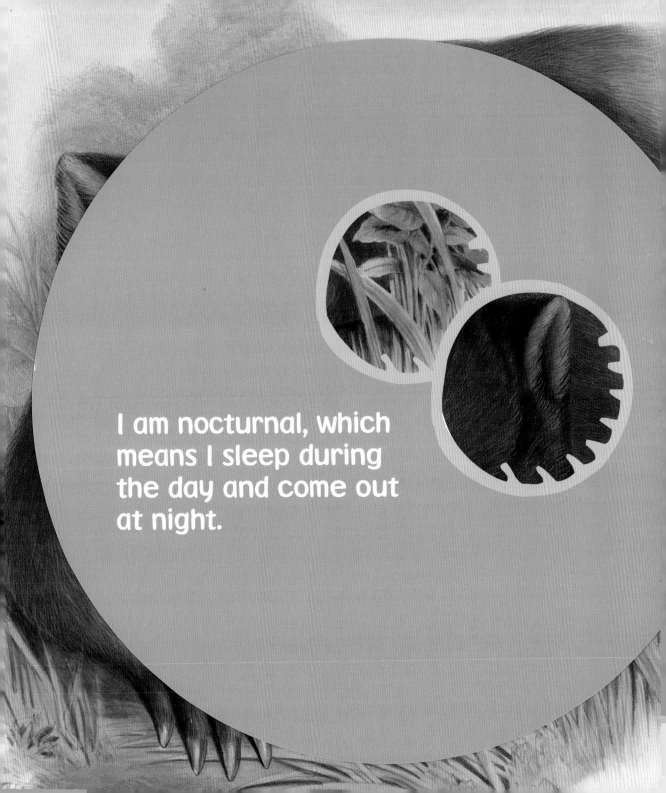

I am nocturnal, which means I sleep during the day and come out at night.

Guess who?

I begin with

I have a hooked beak,
which helps me to
open my food.

Guess who?

I begin with

I move around by hopping and my tail helps me to balance.

Guess who?

I begin with

I make a loud
screeching noise.

Guess who?

I begin with

I am covered with
sharp spines.

Guess who?

I begin with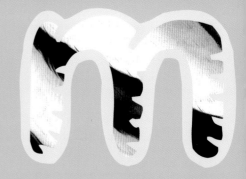

I have black and white feathers.

Guess who?

I begin with

I hang upside down in a tree during the day.

Guess who?

I begin with

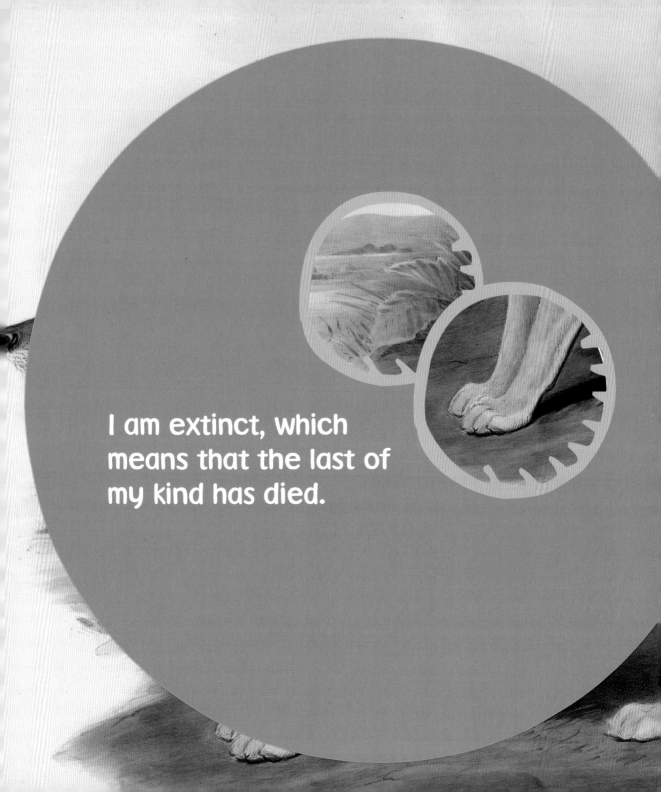

I am extinct, which means that the last of my kind has died.

John Gould

John Gould was born in Dorset, England, on 14 September 1804. His early interest in natural history led to his appointment in 1827 as curator and preserver to the museum of the Zoological Society of London.

Despite his enduring reputation as one of the great names in ornithological art, he was not a gifted artist. Gould employed a group of artists, including his wife Elizabeth, to transform his rough sketches into detailed illustrations and he supervised the printing and hand-colouring of each plate. The resulting meticulously crafted illustrations were collected into a series of luxury publications that appealed to the interests of a wide and moneyed audience including the aristocracy and gentleman scholars.

Gould came to Australia in 1838 with the intention of recording the richly varied birdlife of the continent for his book *The Birds of Australia*. During this visit, his interest was piqued by the extraordinary mammalian life he encountered and he 'conceived the idea of devoting a portion of my attention to the mammalian class of its extraordinary fauna', which resulted in *The Mammals of Australia*, published in 1863.

The Collection

Natural history is richly represented in the Library's collection. With regard to the work of John Gould, the Library holds several of his works including *The Mammals of Australia* and a full set of the first edition of *The Birds of Australia* (which was published in 36 parts over eight years from 1840–48). The Library's Pictures Collection holds a total of 179 key plates, also known as pattern plates, for the books of mammals and birds. These plates were used as colour models for the hand-colouring of the printed plates for publication.

The National Library is the country's largest reference library and it collects a variety of material from manuscripts, maps and music to pictures, online publications, oral histories and ephemera (programs, catalogues, posters, leaflets, etc.). It holds over nine million items in total.

You can see some of these items online at www.nla.gov.au.

2.   3.   4.   5.

7.   8.   9.   10.

hn Gould (1804–1881)
ala (*Phascolarctos cinereus*}
produced from volume 1 of
*e Mammals of Australia: in
ree volumes* 1863
ustralian Collection,
ı.aus-f10032

hn Gould (1804–1881)
eat red kangaroo
sphranter rufus)
produced from volume 2 of
*e Mammals of Australia: in
ree volumes* 1863
ustralian Collection,
ı.aus-f10032

hn Gould (1804–1881)
ombat (*Phascolomys wombat*)
produced from volume 1 of
*e Mammals of Australia: in
ree volumes* 1863
ustralian Collection,
ı.aus-f10032

4. John Gould (1804–1881)
Echidna (*Echidna setosa*)
Reproduced from volume 1 of
*The Mammals of Australia: in
three volumes* 1863
Australian Collection,
nla.aus-f10032

5. John Gould (1804–1881)
Thylacinus
(*Thylacinus cynocephalus*)
Reproduced from volume 1 of
*The Mammals of Australia: in
three volumes* 1863
Australian Collection,
nla.aus-f10032

6. John Gould (1804–1881)
Spectacled flying fox
(*Pteropus conspicillatus*)
Reproduced from volume 3 of
*The Mammals of Australia: in
three volumes* 1863
Australian Collection,
nla.aus-f10032

7. John Gould (1804–1881)
White magpie
(*Gymnorhina organicum*)
Reproduced from volume 2
of *The Birds of Australia: in
seven volumes* 1848
Australian Collection,
nla.aus-f4773-2-s104

8. John Gould (1804–1881)
Emu
(*Dromaius novae-hollandiae*)
Reproduced from volume 6
of *The Birds of Australia: in
seven volumes* 1848
Australian Collection,
nla.aus-f4773-6-s7

9. John Gould (1804–1881)
Sulphur-crested cockatoo
(*Cacatua galerita: Vieill*)
Reproduced from volume 5
of *The Birds of Australia: in
seven volumes* 1848
Australian Collection,
nla.aus-f4773-5-s7

10. John Gould (1804–1881)
King lory
(*Aprosmictus scapulatus*)
Reproduced from volume 5
of *The Birds of Australia: in
seven volumes* 1848
Australian Collection,
nla.aus-f4773-5-s39

Published by the National Library of Australia
Canberra ACT 2600

© National Library of Australia 2007

Reprinted 2007, 2009

National Library of Australia Cataloguing-in-Publication entry

Hall, Susan, 1961– .

Guess who? : A lift-the-flap book about Australian wildlife

For pre-schoolers.
ISBN 978-0-642-27658-2.

1. Animals - Australia - Pictorial works - Juvenile
literature. 2. Flap books. 3. Toy and movable books.
I. National Library of Australia. II. Title.

591.994

Designer: Natalie Webb
Editorial researcher: Rebecca Whitton
Printed in China by Australian Book Connection

The National Library of Australia would like to thank the early childhood
educators and the children at the North Curtin Preschool, Canberra, and
Lee Newton of the RSPCA for their help with this publication.

Cover image: John Gould (1804–1881) Koala (*Phascolarctos cinereus*)
Reproduced from volume 1 of John Gould's *The Mammals of Australia: in
three volumes* 1863 Australian Collection, nla.aus-f10032